T0083295

The Developing

Artist

PIANO SONATINAS

BOOK ONE   Early Intermediate

A COMPREHENSIVE,
WELL-GRADED SERIES
OF AUTHENTIC
KEYBOARD SONATINAS.

Compiled and edited by

Nancy and Randall Faber

Production: Frank & Gail Hackinson
Production Coordinator: Marilyn Cole
Cover: Terpstra Design, San Francisco
Engraving: GrayBear Music Company, Hollywood, Florida
Printer: Vicks

PIANO ADVENTURES®

ISBN 978-1-61677-110-2

Copyright © 1995 by Dovetree Productions, Inc.
c/o FABER PIANO ADVENTURES, 3042 Creek Drive, Ann Arbor, MI 48101
International Copyright Secured.   All Rights Reserved.   Printed in U.S.A.
WARNING: The music, text, design, and graphics in this publication are
protected by copyright law. Any duplication is an infringement of U.S. copyright law.

UNDERSTANDING MUSICAL FORM

Musical *form* is a way of organizing or structuring music.

Composers of sonatas and sonatinas (little sonatas) have written hundreds of pieces with new and different themes (melodies). However, composers usually used only a few musical forms over and over to give structure to their compositions. Imagine a baker baking hundreds of different cakes, but always using the same set of cake pans. Similarly, a composer can create many different pieces using a single musical form.

The following forms are common in early-level classical sonatinas. You and your teacher may wish to refer to this page as you study the sonatinas in this book.

Binary (2-part) form or AB form

The simplest musical form is one section of music followed by another: **section A** followed by **section B.** Each section usually has a repeat sign.
This 2-part (binary) form can be shown like this:

$$\| : \ \mathbf{A} \ : \| : \ \mathbf{B} \ : \|$$

Rounded binary form

This is still 2-part form, but with an interesting feature. In rounded binary form, the theme from section **A** returns *within* the **B** section. It can be shown like this:

$$\| : \ \mathbf{A} \ : \| : \ \mathbf{B} \ (\mathrm{A}) \ : \|$$

Ternary (3-part) form or ABA form

Ternary means 3-parts: **section A, section B,** and the return of **section A.** Ternary form is common in slow, lyric second movements. This 3-part form can be shown like this:

$$\mathbf{A} \quad \mathbf{B} \quad \mathbf{A}$$

Teacher's Note:
Sonata-allegro form only applies to longer, more advanced sonatinas.
Consequently, it is not introduced until Book 2 of this sonatina series.

Table Of Contents

The practice warm-ups in this book will help you play the more difficult spots in each sonatina.
(Words are included to help you learn the music, but need not be sung.)

Your teacher may have you practice each warm-up thoroughly before playing the sonatina hands together.

Practice Warm-ups

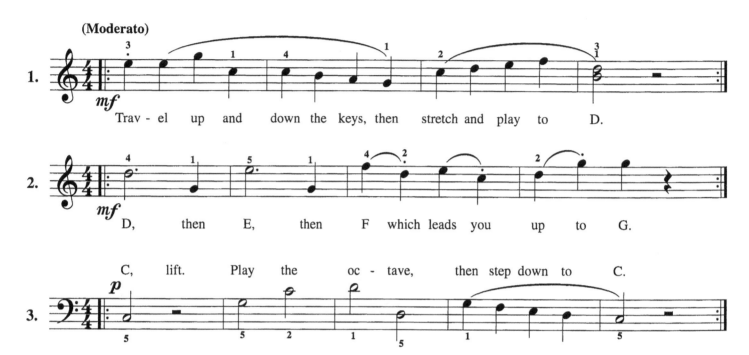

1. Trav - el up and down the keys, then stretch and play to D.

2. D, then E, then F which leads you up to G.

C, lift. Play the oc - tave, then step down to C.

3.

Sonatina in C
(First movement)

Cornelius Gurlitt
(1820-1901)

legato

*Moderato means _____

Exploring the Score: This sonatina has two sections (**A** and **B**) which repeat.

- Label section **A** and section **B** in your music.

- Then point out where the opening theme (**A**) returns within the **B** Section.

2-part form is called **binary form**. ‖: **A** :‖: **B** :‖

When the opening theme returns in the B Section, the form is **rounded binary**.

‖: **A** :‖: **B** (A) :‖

- Is this sonatina in binary or rounded binary form? _____

(you write)

6

Practice Warm-ups

(Allegretto)

1.

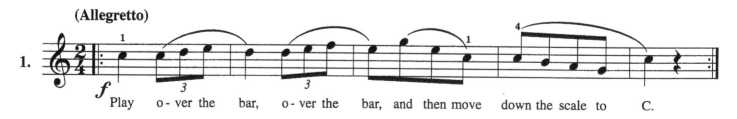

f Play o-ver the bar, o-ver the bar, and then move down the scale to C.

2.

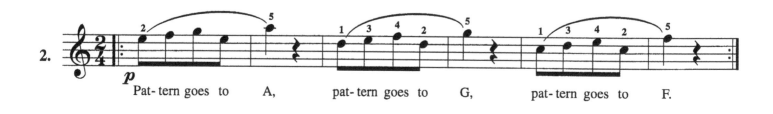

p Pat-tern goes to A, pat-tern goes to G, pat-tern goes to F.

3.

mf I know some-where there's an oc - tave here.

Sonatina in C

William Duncombe
(18th Century)

Allegretto*

move L.H.
quickly

5

***Allegretto** means _____

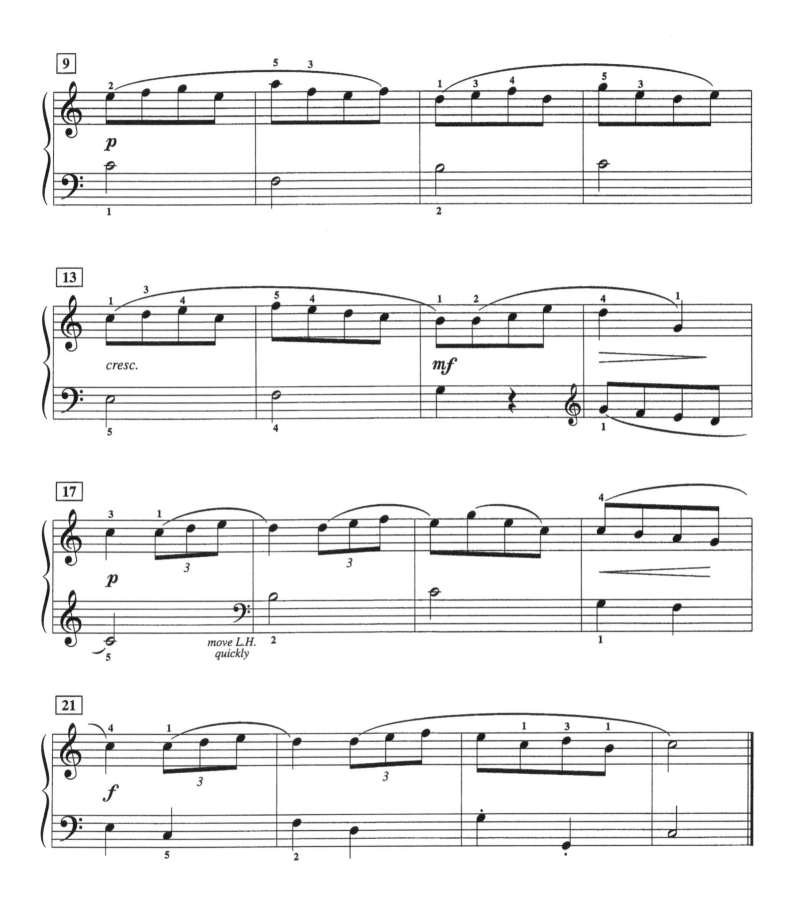

Exploring the Score: This sonatina has 3 sections: **A**, **B**, and the return of **A**.

A B A form is also called **ternary form**.

• Can you find and label each section in your music?

Practice Warm-ups

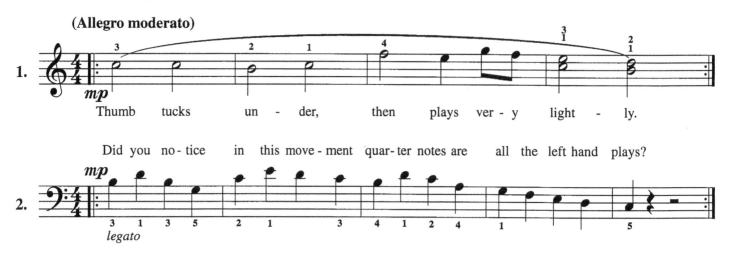

Sonatina
Op. 57, No. 1

Albert Biehl
(1835-1899)

Allegro moderato means _____

Exploring the Score: Sometimes a phrase is repeated with a slight change.

- Find two variations (slight changes) of the first phrase.
  (Hint: The first phrase is measures 1-4).

Practice Warm-ups

(Allegro grazioso)

1.

F, go to E, go to D, go to C, then you play the lead-ing tone and end on C.

(Notice this L.H. warm-up is in the treble clef.)

Gent - ly mov - ing up and down. Lift, drop, lift.

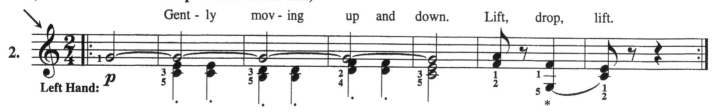

2.

Left Hand: *p*

*Technique Hint: Connect the bottom notes (G to C) while the thumb moves quickly from F down to E.

Allegro grazioso*   **(Second Movement)**

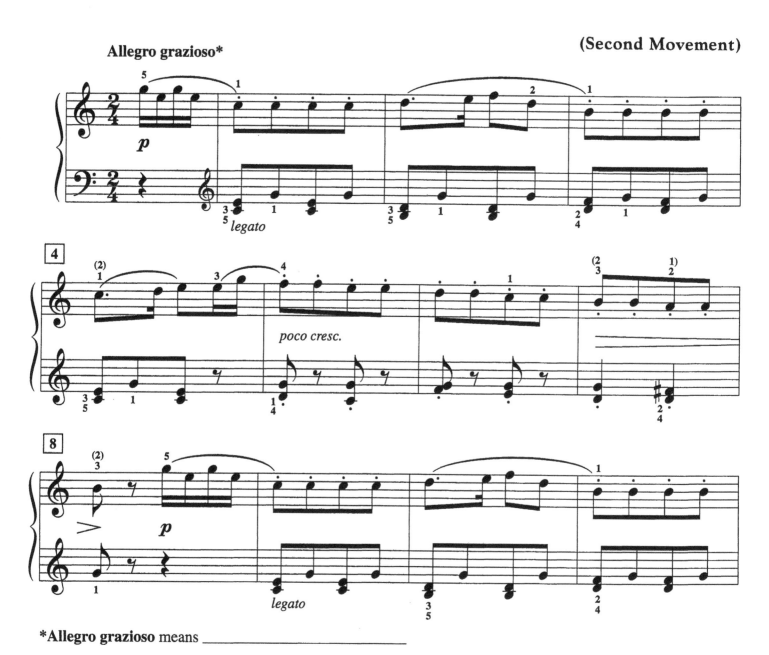

legato

poco cresc.

legato

***Allegro grazioso** means _____

Exploring the Score: Can you find a variation of measures 12-16 later in the piece.

Practice Warm-ups

*Technique Hint: Left hand thumb goes smoothly under when the hand is slanting left.

Sonatina in D

Tat'iana Salutrinskaya

Allegro*

ƒ joyfully

Allegro means _____

Exploring the Score: Themes can be restated beginning on a different tone of the scale.

- Where does the opening theme begin on **step 5** of the D scale? *measure* ____

- Where does it reappear on **step 1** (D) one octave higher? *measure* ____

Practice Warm-ups

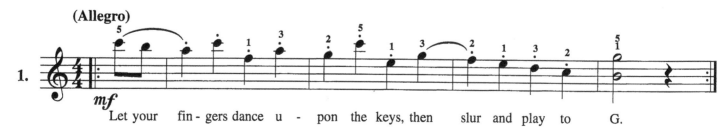

(Allegro)

1.

mf
Let your fin - gers dance u - pon the keys, then slur and play to G.

2.

p   *f*
Play a four - note pat - tern that will lead you up to C.

(Notice this L.H. warm-up is in the treble clef.)

Thumb holds. Thumb holds. Thumb holds. It's the end!

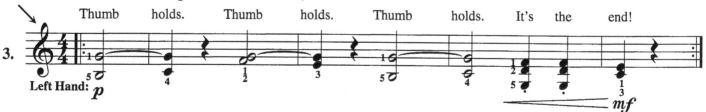

3.

Left Hand: *p*   *mf*

Sonatina in C

Albert Biehl
(1835-1899)

Allegro*

mp

4

mf

*Allegro means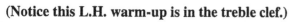

Exploring the Score: An ending section is called a **coda**.

This sonatina has a 5-measure coda.

• Find and label the coda in your music.

(for the Czerny Sonatina on p.18)

Practice Warm-ups

Practice at slower tempos, gradually working up to an *Allegretto*.

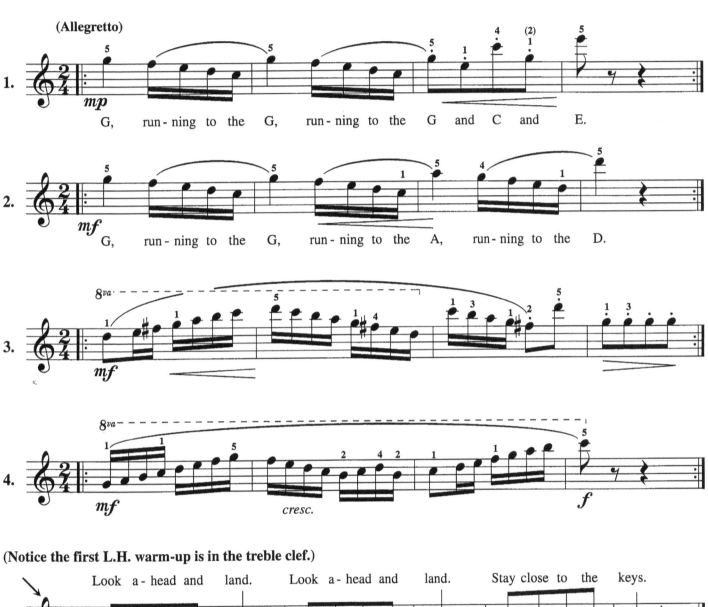

1. G, run-ning to the G, run-ning to the G and C and E.

2. G, run-ning to the G, run-ning to the A, run-ning to the D.

(Notice the first L.H. warm-up is in the treble clef.)

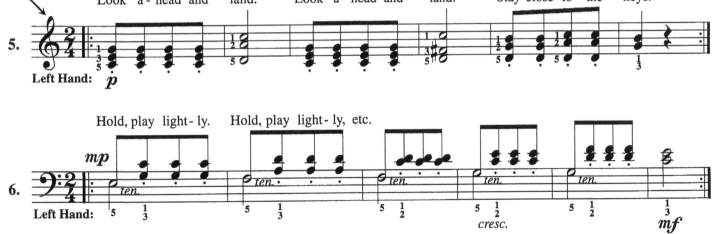

5. Look a-head and land. Look a-head and land. Stay close to the keys.

Left Hand: *p*

6. Hold, play light-ly. Hold, play light-ly, etc.

Left Hand:

Sonatina
Op. 792, No. 8

Carl Czerny
(1791-1857)

*Allegretto means _____

Exploring the Score: Is the form of this movement **binary** (A B) or **ternary** (A B A)?

_____

(you write)

20

Teacher's Note: The first two warm-ups are written in augmentation (longer note values) to help with the rhythm.

Practice Warm-ups

(Second Movement)

*Andante means _____

Exploring the Score: Circle the form of this sonatina:

Binary

‖: **A** :‖‖: **B** :‖

Rounded binary

‖: **A** :‖‖: **B** (A) :‖

Practice Warm-up

Many concert artists practice **hands alone** for correct **fingering**, **articulation**, and **dynamics**.
Use this practice technique to help you learn this movement.

(Third Movement)

Exploring the Score: Circle the form of this movement:

Binary	Rounded binary	Ternary
‖: A :‖‖: B :‖	‖: A :‖‖: B (A) :‖	A B A

(for the Attwood Sonatina in G on p.24)

Practice Warm-ups

1.

2.

3.

4.

5.

*See Technique Hint on p. 10.

Sonatina in G

Thomas Attwood
(1765-1838)

* The slur notation indicates that the D (downbeat of measure 5) both ends the preceding phrase and begins the new phrase.

Exploring the Score: A passage which connects two sections is called a **transition.**

- The form of this piece is **A B A**. Can you find the transition between Section B and the return to Section A?

- Your teacher may ask you to label each section in your music.

Practice Warm-ups

Minuetto
(Second Movement)

*Andante means _____

Exploring the Score: Circle the form of this movement:

Binary	Rounded binary	Ternary
‖: **A** :‖‖: **B** :‖	‖: **A** :‖‖: **B** (A) :‖	**A** **B** **A**

Practice Warm-up

Remember, a warm-up for success is practicing **hands alone** for correct **fingering**, **articulation**, and **dynamics.** Use this "success warm-up" to help learn this final movement.

Rondo
(Third Movement)

*This appoggiatura may be played quickly, as a grace note, on the beat. (See definition of long and short appoggiaturas on p. 30.)

Exploring the Score: Circle the form of this movement:

Binary   Rounded binary   Ternary

‖: A :‖‖: B :‖   ‖: A :‖‖: B (A) :‖   A B A

DICTIONARY OF MUSICAL TERMS

DYNAMIC MARKS

pp	*p*	*mp*	*mf*	*f*	*ff*
pianissimo	*piano*	*mezzo piano*	*mezzo forte*	*forte*	*fortissimo*
very soft	soft	medium soft	medium loud	loud	very loud

crescendo
play gradually louder

diminuendo
play gradually softer

TEMPO MARKS

Andante	*Moderato*	*Allegretto*	*Allegro*
"walking speed" (slower than Moderato)	moderate tempo	rather fast, cheerful	fast and lively

SIGN	TERM	DEFINITION
	Alberti bass	A left hand accompaniment which outlines the notes of a chord using the pattern: bottom-top-middle-top. The *Alberti bass* was popularized during the Classic period (approximately 1750 to 1830).
	Allegro moderato	Moderately fast.
	appoggiatura	An ornamental note that is played on the beat and moves stepwise up or down. There can be long and short appoggiaturas. The long appoggiatura equally shares the value of the main note in most cases. The short appoggiatura is played quickly, as a grace note, into the main note.
	a tempo	Return to the beginning tempo (speed).
	binary form	A musical form with 2 sections (Section A and Section B). Each section usually repeats. ‖: A :‖: B :‖
	cantabile	Singing.
	Coda	Ending section. (A short *Coda* is called a *Codetta*.)
	D.C. al Fine	*Da Capo al Fine.* Return to the beginning and play until *Fine* (end).
	dolce	Sweetly.
⌢	*fermata*	Hold this note longer than usual.
	Fine	End here.
	form	Musical form refers to the overall structure of a piece.
	grazioso	Gracefully.
	legato	Smoothly, connected.
	marcato	Marked; each note well articulated.
	minuetto	Italian for "minuet." A minuet is a stately dance in $\frac{3}{4}$ time.

SIGN	TERM	DEFINITION
8va	*ottava*	Play one octave higher than written. When written below the bass staff, it means to play one octave lower.
	phrase	A musical idea. Think of a phrase as a "musical sentence." It is shown in the music with a slur, also called a phrase mark.
	poco	A little. For example, *poco rit.* means a little ritard.
rit.	*ritardando*	Gradually slow down.
	rounded binary form	Two-part form (**A B**) with a special feature: the theme from Section A returns within Section B. ‖ **A** ‖ **B** (A) ‖
	rondo form	The form for a piece which has a recurring A Section. Ex. A B A C A
	score	The written music.
	sempre	Always. For example, *sempre staccato* means to continue playing staccato.
	senza	Without. For example, *senza Ped.* means without pedal.
	slur	Connect the notes under or above a slur.
	sonata	An instrumental piece; usually with 3 movements.
	sonatina	A little sonata. Sonatinas can have one, two, but seldom more than three movements.
	staccato	Play notes marked *staccato* detached; disconnected.
	tenuto mark	Hold this note its full value. Press gently into the key.
	tempo	The speed of the music.
ten.	*tenuto*	Hold the note its full value.
	ternary	A musical form with 3 sections: **A B A**.
	theme	Melody. A piece may have several themes.
	transition	A passage which connects two sections.
	triplet	3 eighth notes to a quarter note beat.
	turn	A musical ornament that "turns" above and below the given note.

ABOUT THE COMPOSERS

Thomas Attwood (1765-1838)

Attwood was an English organist and composer. He studied with Mozart who wrote teaching pieces for him. Attwood was co-founder and conductor of the London Philharmonic Society.

Albert Biehl (1835-1899)

Biehl was a German pianist and composer who wrote many light parlor pieces and teaching pieces.

Carl Czerny (1791-1857)

Czerny was born in Vienna. He was a student of Beethoven and became a famous teacher of piano. His pupils included the famous pianist Franz Liszt. Czerny is well-known for his collections of piano studies and exercises.

William Duncombe (18th century)

Duncombe was an English composer and harpsichordist. He was also a teacher who composed and compiled a set of lessons for the keyboard.

Cornelius Gurlitt (1820-1901)

As a young man, Gurlitt studied in Copenhagen, Denmark, and travelled throughout Germany, Bohemia, Austria and Italy. He taught at the Hamburg Conservatory and composed choral, orchestral, and keyboard music. He is now best known for his teaching pieces for the piano.

Tat'iana Saliutrinskaya

Saliutrinskaya was a Russian composer known for her orchestral compositions.